*ISBN: 979-8-89238-117-8 (Paperback)*

*ISBN: 979-8-89238-119-2 Ebook)*



*Disclaimer: This is a work of fiction. Any resemblance to actual events or persons, living or dead, is entirely coincidental.*

*Editing by Book Baby*

*Illustrated by Sahir Hussin*

*Self- Publish by Shareka Thomas*

*Prom-ise*

*A Declaration or assurance that one will do a particular thing or that a particular thing will happen.*

Promises are worse than lies. You don't just make them BELIEVE; you also make them HOPE!

-Marilyn Monroe

What comes to mind when I say a broken household? For some people that are not so familiar with this subject it is a family in which one parent is absent. Does a broken home affect the children? Yes, it surely does, these affects sometimes cause health issues, lack of self-confidence, irrational fears and anxiety, anti- social behavior, nightmares, depression, suicidal thoughts, and academic development.

Parents, have you ever had to explain divorce, splitting up or just can't answer why he/ she isn't present in your life to a child that wasn't asked to be born but needs unconditional love and guidance?

They say when you are important to another person, that person will always find a way to make time for you. No excuses, no lies, no broken promises. Did you know promises are worse than lies? So, I've experienced time after time. Promises always make others hope for something that you're not sure you can even give, why do people do this? Take my dad for an instant, when I tell you he's the king of broken promises I mean that. I have experienced disappointment after disappointment to the point of no return where numbness is an understatement evolving my emotion.

How do we break this awful cycle? I know life is about making choices and we all are struggling with something but sometimes you must have the mindset that when you can't control what's happening, challenge yourself to control the way to respond to what's happening.

Growing up in a broken family I've learned to accept what is, let go of what I thought it should be and have faith in all it could be. This was no easy process but vital to my growth as a young man. I refused to be a product of my circumstances and I hope my story can help you make that decision as well. No, we don't ask to be born but when we are born the world becomes a little brighter. Like I said earlier my dad is the king of broken promises, so I don't trust words anymore, I trust action.

Alone in my secret cave where mom couldn't hear my sniffles, I blew my nose as quietly as possible. "How dare I shed a tear? I promised myself that I wouldn't cry this time," I threw my piece of tissue at my best friend Ted. "He always let me down! Every single time," I cried hugging Ted while I fell asleep in my secret cave.

"Good morning, Courage! I see you fell asleep in your tent again," Mom smiled at me and Ted. "Mom it's not a tent it's a secret cave, I only told you where it was located because you're my mom" I gave her a serious stare. "Well, if I knew that you would sleep more in your secret cave than your bed, I would have left your bed at the store" mom chuckled. "How about you and Ted come join me for some breakfast" Mom suggested.

"So son, when are you going to stop dragging ted around everywhere you go?" mom questioned as she made my plate. "Mom sometimes Ted needs some fresh air, he hates it when I leave him alone all day" I sat Ted at the table beside me. "Honey I truly understand that ted's your best friend, but baby ted is a stuff animal, you're going to have to learn how to do things without him, because when school starts tomorrow you cannot take him with you, you're in the first grade now son so you cannot bring toys to school anymore" mom explained. "

"That's not fair mom ted is more than just a stuffed animal, he's really my friend. He knows all my secrets, he watches over me while I sleep, and he's the best listener I know" I defended my friendship. "Well son I understand why Ted is so important to you, but like I said someday you will have to learn how to do things without him" Mom patiently repeated herself "Oh yeah like dad? "I surprised my mother with my outburst. "That's absolutely correct, Courage one day you will look around and I won't be here your dad won't be here and Ted won't be here" she said calmly.

"I hear you mom, but I think Ted will always have my back, he never lets me down and he always keeps his promises unlike other people," I picked up Ted so I could go to my cave, I needed to vent badly. "Well son I know why ted is so important to you, it was the last thing your father gave you before moving out of town and I know your father promises you a lot of things that he never follows through with but like my mom once told me you can't control other people action or sometimes what's happens to you, you can only control how you respond to it Courage" Mom always knew how to explain things to make me feel better when she seen me losing control over my emotion.

"I hear you mom; may I be excused from the table now?" If I had to wait another second, tears were going to be all over this table. "Yes, you may son, but try and remember sometimes it's not about what or who is missing, what's really important is what you already have. Do you know why I named you courage? You were supposed to be named after your father's but when I laid eyes on you, I thought about all the things in life that would frighten you and all the things that would try and change you from becoming your best version. I had to name you Courage as a reminder to yourself because it's going to take a lot of bravery to be yourself in a world that is constantly trying to make you into something that you are not" she patted my shoulder.

“I hear you mom, trying to end the conversation” I hurried to my room ready to explode. “Did you hear that crap?” I yelled at Ted once we reached the secret cave. “Why is she making excuses for him huh? She doesn’t get any days off being a mother but it's okay for my dad too?”

I waited for Ted to respond but I knew he never said much but always listened like he cared. “Ted’s mom says you're just a stuffed animal, but I know you're real! I just need your help right about now my dear friend” I fell asleep holding ted just hoping that he would say something.

That night was very strange. I was woken by a bright sparkly light while I slept in my cave. “Can somebody please turn off the lights?” I said, barely keeping my eyes open. “No, I cannot,” a strange voice answered back. After hearing that response, I started to panic. I was too afraid to open my eyes “It’s okay Courage it’s just me” The voice started to whisper. For some weird reason something inside me told me to trust the little friendly voice and I began to slowly opened my eyes and there was ted standing over me shining so bright, I instantly got afraid and closed them back “You’re not real” I tried to convince myself that my stuff animal was not standing up by himself and most definitely not talking to me “But I am Courage, last thing I remember you saying in our secret cave was you needed me, where here I am buddy how may I help!” Ted asked with a smile.

“Okay Ted if you’re real what is our secret code to the cave? “I knew if Ted was real, he would know the code because you cannot enter the secret cave without the code. “You can’t keep a good dog down? Am I correct right? A scene from your favorite movie Courage that was way too easy?” Ted waited for his friend to believe in him. “Oh my god, oh my god it’s really you ted it’s really you” I knew only my best friend could answer that question.

"The one and only" Ted took a bow knowing his dear friend was starting to believe him. "But how?" I was cut off by Ted signaling me to be quiet. "Don't you even say it, friends of mine remember this cave is a secret cave and a magical one when you believe it," Ted tried to explain. See you believed in me and that's why I'm here, didn't you call me for help?" Ted questioned "Yes I did" wondering what I got myself into "well here I am buddy, what kind of friend would I be if I didn't show up when you needed me the most! I hear tomorrow is a big day for you, my little first grader. Wow you show are really getting old on me Courage," Ted smiled at the memories of him and courage adventures while Courage was a little baby.

"Well Ted it's my dad, he promised me that he would take me to school on my first day but called yesterday making up some excuse about his work," I said sadly. "Oh, I remember that conversation yesterday when you were so upset, but is that just it? I feel like you have a deeper issue with your dad, it can't just be him missing one day, right? Ted already knew the answer but needed Courage to express himself the best way he could.

“You're right Ted it’s more! First, he leaves me and my mom and gets a new house and a new family and then he stops coming around or getting me once he has another child and he never ever keeps his promises Ted” I started to cry. “Last year at graduation he didn’t even show up Ted, everyone had their mom’s and dad’s clapping in the stands but where was mine? I even pretended to act sick, so I didn’t have to go on stage until he made it but once they called the last kid, I knew then he wasn’t going to show up. All my friends introduced me to their parents, but I was too ashamed because out of all my friends my dad was the only one not there.” I stopped to take a breath.

“That’s not it! He signed me up for baseball but never comes to my games. I worked so hard last season I hit a home run in the championship game, but I couldn’t even be happy because the one person I wanted to see me do it was nowhere in sight. Can you just imagine winning a big game and all the players’ dad are holding their sons in the air and here I am looking at my mom who just doesn’t know what to say besides great job. I’m not sure what I did to make him hate me, I don’t care about his money, I don’t even care if we go places. I just want my dad back” I cried even more.

nter

Ted listened carefully until I was finished then responded, "First things first your dad doesn't hate you, Courage! A lot of kids experience broken homes like yourself, maybe not your closest friends but I'm sure you have classmates that're either missing a mom or dad. I do feel like they could have sat you down to explain the immediate changes you were going to experience but maybe you were just too young back then to comprehend that,".

"Look Courage I'm your best friend so I'm going to tell you what most people wouldn't say but sometimes life isn't fair. We don't get to choose who our parents or siblings are. We don't get to choose where we are born or the condition or environment, so you just have to make the best of what you have. Picture this, just like you have a mom who cooks and cleans and tells you everything is going to be okay, there's someone out there in the world who doesn't have that at all. Of course, it would be nice to have a mom and dad but how nice would it be to have neither one because someone in the world has no mom or no dad" Ted continued.

"My point is I really can't tell you why your dad isn't around, only he can explain that, but I will show you how to deal with your mindset in the meantime. My mother always told me if you want to stop feeling sorry for yourself listen to someone else's problem because someone out in the world always has it worse than you do. Take me for an instant. I was taken from my mom, put into a scary big place where people would come visit and play with me and leave me there. I didn't have my mom or my dad. I only had the memories of her warning me for this day to come. My Mom told me that one day someone was going to take me away and place me inside a big store where I would find my new mommy or daddy. Can you imagine how scary that was for me? I sat on that shelf for months wondering why no one wanted me" Ted face showed sadness as he continued.

"Until that day" Ted smiled "until what?" I was feeling like I missed something. "Until the day your father came into the store and blessed me with the most precious gift you Courage. See I never understood my mother when she said if you can't do anything about it let it go, don't be a prisoner to things you can't change. I had to learn how to accept things for what they were and know that the best is yet to come and that's what you must do. You must start practicing gratitude to condition your mind to be grateful for what you already have because that's all what really matters anyways," Ted patted my shoulder as he continued.

"Now don't think for one second that little voices in my head didn't tell me all kinds of ugly little things that weren't true while I sat in the store thinking this might be the day. Picture trying to be as positive as you can, but you have a voice going against that saying no one wants you, which had me questioning my existence until your dad came inside the store that day and chose me to be your new best friend. At first, I was nervous because of what the other teddy bears would say in the store. Sometimes people bring you home just to bring you back; I was hoping that you would need me like I needed you because in the car ride to your home your dad prayed over me like he needed my help. I didn't understand that day in the car until I was placed into your arms, and you squeezed me to death. I knew right then not only did I need you, but you needed me too," Ted hugged me so tight.

"So just know sometimes your circle might decrease in size but increase in value, personally I would choose value over size any day. For example, I could have five fake friends just to say I have a lot of friends or just one real friend that I know has my back at the end of the day. We sometimes create our own heartbreaks through expectation as my mom would put it even for our parents. Come on now! Be for real how do we even know what's a good parent from a bad parent or what's the right thing to do or the wrong thing to do life has no blueprint or a cheat sheet to a perfect life," Ted explained.

"Courage, I get tomorrow is a very important day for you and I understand in your perfect world everyone that you loved would be there if you could have it your way, but friend life doesn't. Work that way, Courage. Sometimes life works the very opposite to what you want or believe should happen then what? Do you just stop living or give up? Absolutely not! Disappointment, unfairness, and heartbreak will all come someday knocking on your door. It's inevitable my friend. One Day back at the store I was told once by another teddy bear that saw me crying that you'll never know how strong you are until being strong is the only choice you have. I used to think to myself why people keep giving me so much advice at the store but now I know it was just wisdom to be passed on from one person to another. I am helping you shift your perspective and someday you can help someone like yourself'," Ted instructed me to stand up.

"If you change the way you look at things, the things you look at will change, you know having the right perspective makes the impossible possible right? I know you can do it my friend because I was once counting all the things that were going wrong versus all the things that were going right for me. For instance, tomorrow is your first day of school, right? When you wake up tomorrow your mother is going to greet you with a warm smile and some encouraging words, your mother is going to cook you something delicious to eat and put you in a hot shower and provide you with clean clothes to wear before taking you to school right?" Ted questioned "Yes that's right" I was cut off.

“My point is your tomorrow is going to look different from someone else's tomorrow, just like you're going to be woken up with love someone is going to have to wake up on their own or by an alarm clock. Just like you’re going to eat those hot pancakes and bacon one of your classmates is going to have to come to school hungry and hoping the cafeteria is still open. You have a hot shower to use and clean clothes to put on but once again a classmate of yours didn’t get to shower today or wasn’t fortunate to have clean clothes available. Your mother will drive you to school tomorrow, walk you to your class and kiss you and tell you to learn something new and have a good day. One of your classmates tomorrow will have to walk all the way to school with no mommy or no daddy. Who’s the blessed one Courage? You once asked me to just say something, well this is that something friend count your blessings not your problems the same things that we take for granted or the same things that others are praying for” Ted fell to the floor like someone unplugged him.

I knew at that moment that he had said all he needed to say, and the rest was all up to me so I just laid beside my best friend smiling at the fact that I knew all along that he was real. “Watch me flip my mindset” I whispered in Ted’s ear before falling to sleep.

The very next day came and just like Ted said Mom greeted me with loving words of encouragement. She cooked my favorite food and had my clean clothes laid out on my bed once I showered. It was too hard not to notice all the things that were working for me. I even saw my mom sneak and put a little love note in my lunch pail. Once I was done getting ready for school mom drove me to school in our nice warm car and as we drove by so many kids, I couldn't help but wonder which kid didn't have the best start like I did.

Once we arrived at the school, I saw all kinds of people bringing kids to school, not just mother's and father's I saw grandmother's I saw brother's and sister's I even saw babysitter doing some dropping off. Mom looked really worried about me as we got closer to my classroom and the parents were saying farewell to their children. I could feel her anxiety rising from the way she was squeezing my hand, so I stopped walking to get attention. "Is everything okay son?" she bent down and looked me straight in the eyes.

"Yes, mom everything is great! I know I had you stressed the other day but I'm okay now, all it took was for a good friend to help me switch my perspective on things. Yes, my dad breaks a lot of promises but mom you have never.

Did my father leave us and start over with a new family, he sure did but that's his lost mom! So, what if my dad doesn't come to my baseball games, you've never missed a single one and you always make sure you bring as much family as possible and one last thing mom so what if he couldn't make it today to send me off to school you always make sure you don't miss anything that's important to me thank you mom I can always count on you" I kissed her before going into class and said I will learn something new and have a wonderful day thanks to you and at that moment the secret cave lit up and Ted smiled and said "I knew you could do it."

# Mindset Fresh Book Collection

*This wonderful book collection is available in two formats. Ebook's (Amazon Kindle) paperback in over 450 book retailers, bookstores, and libraries all over the US and other territories, so make sure you visit your nearby bookstore in person or shop online.*

**Litty & The Giant**
**Print ISBN** *978-1-63848-383-0*
**Ebook ISBN** *978-1-63877-969-8*

**Blue & Wormy Self-Love Stroll to School**
**Print ISBN** *978-1-0879-8363-9*
**Ebook ISBN** *978-1-0879-8360-8*

**My Favorite Apple Tree**
**Print ISBN** *979-8-88589-637-5*
**Ebook ISBN** 979-8-88589-638-2

**On My Journey 2 Greatness**
**Print ISBN** *978-1-63848-386-1*
**Ebook ISBN** *978-1-63901-912-0*

**Mindset Fresh 31 Day Reflection Journal**
**Print ISBN** 978-1-the 63877-967-1
**Ebook ISBN** 978-1-63877-969-8

**Mindset Fresh Kid's Reflection Journal**
**Print ISBN** 978-1-63877-955-1
**Ebook ISBN** 978-1-63877-956-8

**My Millionaire Routine**
**Print ISBN** 978--8-88796-879-7
**Ebook ISBN** 978-8-88796-870-4

*Shareka Thomas challenges people of all ages to live out their own "Phenomenal Self". Her motivation comes from childhood experiences, as there were times where she struggled with self-doubt, fear, and adversity. Over the years she has overcome those barriers through prayer, listening to motivational speakers, changing her perspective, facing her fears, and speaking nothing but positivity into her life existence.*

*She loves to share her story and encourage others to discover their superpower and climb endless stairs of possibilities. She believes that if you walk by faith and not by sight nothing is impossible. If you can dream it, you can achieve it.*

www.ingramcontent.com/pod-product-compliance
Ingram Content Group UK Ltd.
Pitfield, Milton Keynes, MK11 3LW, UK
UKHW061949290726
14090UKWH00021B/1147

9 798892 381178